# Bigger Than A Bump

Indigo Pascall

# *Table of Contents*

# *Chapter 1*

## THE PIVOT

At a point in your life, you've felt like you weren't enough. Maybe that feeling was not being smart enough, slim enough, tall enough, whatever your "not enough" was, it held you back from loving yourself completely. My "not enough" was not being pretty enough. If you are familiar with this feeling, you know that not feeling attractive is like a stubborn stain on your clothes. A stain you'll do anything to get out or cover-up. Not being confident in your appearance is a feeling that haunts you every day because it's not like you can wake up and look like someone else. "Self-love" is a term we see and hear all the time from parents, friends, social media, and so on. Wikipedia defines self-love as the regard for one's own well-being and happiness. While that is all true, to me, self-love is the "chin up" in your walk, the assurance in your talk, and the vibrance in your energy. Self-love isn't something you buy. It isn't something you open a book and learn. It starts well, obviously, with self. Allow me to dive into my personal struggles with self-love. How I lost it, how I explored other avenues to find it, how the lack of it affected many relationships, and how it overall left me with physical and mental scars I'm still trying to eliminate.

## *Where'd It Go?*

This dark cloud began following me in the sixth grade. Young, right? I know. Those middle school years are tricky. That transition from child to adolescence is real! Real awkward! You go from being the confident, unbothered kid that didn't care about the opinions of others to waiting up for a "to be honest" post on MySpace or Facebook (for my fellow millennials) from middle schoolers to find out if they think you're cute or not. It gets weird. Every day I went to school, I overheard the middle school drama of who liked who, who kissed who, who asked who for their numbers, and I was always overlooked. I watched how comfortable everyone else was with how they looked and I remember thinking to myself, Am I missing something?

When I was a kid, I was a confident kid. I strutted on and off the stage as a dancer, singer, and performer. Any extracurricular activity my parents could think of, I was in it. Dance classes, acting classes, youth groups, church choir, spelling bees, I was a true creative. These activities took confidence! So I knew I had it. I was the diva who waved to her parents in the crowd at every dance recital. I was the leader chosen for solos and lead roles. However, somewhere along the way, I stopped loving the way I looked, which ultimately stripped away my confidence little by little.

## *Stepping into Womanhood*

I didn't just wake up one day and not love the way I looked. On April 16, 2009, a day I'll never forget, I had just ended a normal day at Howard M. Phifer Middle School. The day was just like any other; same old teachers, same old students, same old small clique I was with every day. It was the sixth grade, nothing was out of the ordinary. Not to mention it was my first year in public school. For anymore who has experienced the transition from private school to public school, it's a real culture shock! I was already the odd ball. While getting off of the school bus to walk one-half block home, I felt this gooey moisture in my underwear. So, when I got home, I went straight to the bathroom and discovered it was happening. Yup, eleven-year-old me was beginning the process the world likes to call "becoming a woman." Wait, I wasn't ready! I knew such little about it. I didn't know about sex, I barely knew about puberty, and now I was to remember my sixth-grade health teacher's lecture. Who pays attention in health class? So, besides the terrible fact that blood rushes through your uterus once a month, the body of a young woman is preparing itself for childbirth. My hips spread a little. Those training bras I literally begged my mom to get me turned into Walmart size 32A cups, and my face, Lord, my face was breaking out left and right! I didn't experience the normal side effects like other young girls. You know, the snappy attitudes, the emotional roller coaster, the weight gain. I didn't even get the cramps! I just got the breakouts. It started kind of innocently. One or two bumps here and there, No biggie, but as I got older, it got much worse. The last time I saw my skin completely clear was in 2009. At those awkward preteen years, kids stick their noses and two cents into something when nobody asked them. Classmates reminded me of what was on my face, as if I didn't look into the mirror. I heard things like, "You've got a pimple" or "Ew, why does your face look like that?" or "You should use ProActiv or something." Family members told me I needed to stop eating junk food, that I needed to drink more water, blah, blah, blah. (Sidenote: Drinking water does nothing for people with cystic acne, but we'll touch on that later.)

It's safe to say that acne shifted my childhood completely. Acne changed me in so many ways. I did not know where it came from and or how to make it stop. At eleven, I didn't know what to do and where to put these feelings of low self-esteem. All I knew was when I looked into the mirror, I hated what stared back at me. That's a heavy feeling for anybody. Acne stripped those last bit of childhood years from me. I tapped into that dark self-doubt place pretty early. There's no commonly right age where self-doubt is okay, but eleven is just early. I wasn't ready for it. My body was still changing, I was still growing. To the average Joe, this may not sound like that big of a deal, but to anyone who has or had acne, trust me, it is. I felt like I had some sort of disease or plague. It was a curse. Throughout my teenage years, I couldn't understand why it wasn't going away! I did everything my peers were doing. I played outside, I was involved, I wasn't doing anything different. Why didn't their faces look like mine? More importantly, why didn't my face look like theirs?

# *Chapter 2*

## TAKING JABS

Being the only one amongst my friends and family members with bad skin got hard to hide. I was still a kid, I didn't want to wear makeup, so I wore little. I didn't want to express how having bad acne made me feel to anybody. Being at school was hard enough so when I was home or around my family members, I just wanted to be free from that dark feeling of being ugly. Ask yourself this question: Are your family members aware of your insecurities and your triggers? Whether you feel self-conscious about your weight, your skin, or your height, do your loved ones know how you feel, or do you keep it all bottled up? In my case, the only person in my family I expressed my genuine feelings about my skin to was my mother. Looking back, I wish I was more expressive to all of my family members, but I just didn't know how to be. What was I supposed to do? Hold a big family meeting and say, "Hey, family, I hate that I suffer from cystic acne and I would appreciate it if you guys didn't comment or stare." Instead, I suffered in silence, which caused my family to make remarks without even knowing they were doing damage to my self-esteem.

## *You've Gotta Speak Up*

Support and understanding of your loved ones are so important. A lot of times, families are even the ones doing the damage. Have you ever walked into a family function and the first greeting from a family member is a critique of your physical appearance? Comments like, "Hey, cousin, you've gained some weight, honey," or "What's going on with your skin, baby?" Note to family members like these: These are not greetings! Just say hello and keep it pushing! I think it is insensitive of anyone to pinpoint someone's flaws when you don't know if this is someone's trigger or how these flaws make that person feel. Family or not, no one should do this.

After returning from college, I gained some weight, which wasn't a painless transition for me.

Before college, I was skinny and had a beautiful athletic frame, so a random forty extra pounds did something to my confidence. I remember when I would come home on breaks from college and my family would grab my little stomach pudge or smack my ass or thighs just to remind me I'd gotten fat. Gee, thanks? Comments like these from family members are so unnecessary! You never know how someone is dealing with something. I had just finished college and like most people, I gained weight! So what? Sure, my "freshman 15" was more of a freshman 25, which turned into a forty-pound gain over four years, but shit, that was my business! I wasn't comfortable with it yet, so getting jabs thrown at me here and there added to my stress. I didn't want nor need anyone to remind me of it! There are so many other examples of my family members picking on my weight and skin.

### *Do you have an outlet?*

There was one person in this world who knew I wasn't happy with myself and that was my mother. Hiding low self-esteem is pretty hard with your mom, but to everyone else, I was a pro. When my brothers or dad came around, I would cover my tears and throw on a smile, but my mom? You know moms with their adamant, soft tone, how could I cover anything from her? My mother's shoulder was always there to cry on. No matter how early it was, how late it was, how tired she was, she was there for me. Back then, my self-esteem was jacked up! I'm talking about getting dressed with the lights off, jacked up. Standing at least five feet away from the mirror so I didn't have to get a close up on my face and flaws kind of jacked up. My mama was always there to lift my head. She made it comfortable for me to confide in her, and if it wasn't for her knowing me so well, I wouldn't have told anybody. I guess a mother knows. Shout out to you, Mommy!

Some people in your life are there to help you through whatever you're going through, like my mommy. Others don't even understand how much something affects you so they don't ask, or, without knowing, they trigger you, like my other family members and friends. With my mom, she talked to me about how this was just a phase and how many kids my age went through this. Every day, she reminded me of my beauty. However, hearing I was beautiful did nothing for my self-esteem. It went through one ear and straight out the other. As much as I wanted to, I couldn't bring myself to believe her every time she told me I was beautiful. My mom taught me that beauty was within and no blemish, scar, or bump defined me. She hugged me and assured me I would not feel like this forever, that it would be over soon. These pep talks were just like the medications I used—a temporary fix. Eventually, the low self-esteem would return.

My face was a sensitive topic for me and some days, I just didn't need anyone to remind of it. Hell, most days I didn't even want anyone to see me. This became hard because, during middle and high school, I had to maintain my role as a student leader. I couldn't let anybody see Indigo cry. Couldn't let them see me down. That was between me and me. Not only was I embarrassed by the bumps, but it was embarrassing for a strong-willed kid like myself to feel this low about herself. I just dealt with it. It drove me crazy. Crying in the bathroom one minute to clean myself up and joking around with my friends the next. I was a ball of confusion and, after a while, tired of faking it. Doing this did a lot of damage because now I know that if I had opened up and expressed myself to someone, I could've gotten this self-esteem thing under control earlier. I could've avoided years of bad days and low self-esteem if I just talked about it. Telling myself to "tighten up" and not show anybody I was hurting within, hurt me in the long run. I come from a household where, even at our lowest moments, we persevere. That's just how my parents raised me, don't let anybody see you down, push through, and make it happen. Many households raise their children with these rituals, and while these lessons are great in some areas of life, it causes us to bury our feelings and we grow up not knowing how to communicate our pain. We release our pain by "letting it out on the field" in sports, hurt our significant others by not knowing how to communicate in our relationships, suppress our feelings by drowning in drugs or alcohol, and take unnecessary paths to escape our pain instead of letting it out and revealing our vulnerability. Why is that? Is it because we don't have anyone to talk to? I know for my Black community, we have this crazy idea that therapy and counseling are for the weak. This generational idea that getting help and talking out our problems is a sign of weakness and is one from which I've suffered.

After battling low self-esteem for over ten years, I am finally letting my guard down and showing people that, for a long time, I was hurting. I am not weak. I'm human! Today I know I don't have to be that superhero and deal with how I feel by myself. We deserve to be happy with ourselves. In this crazy world we're living in, it's the least we can do…for ourselves. So keep your comments to yourself, family and friends, I know I have terrible skin. No need for the reminder.

*Chapter 3*

## TREATMENTS

Having acne doesn't look or feel the same to everyone. Everyone's bodies are different. What works for me may not work for others, and vice versa. Our bodies are uniquely made for just us. For example, I have extremely dry skin. Even when I moisturize my body and face, I often need a second layer of moisture because it's so dry. However, my mom has oily skin so we don't share the same skincare products in the house. As a disclaimer, just because the products I had used for my skin hadn't worked for me doesn't mean they are not effective products. I used just about every over-the-counter product, but nothing worked for my particular skin. The hardest emotional battle was trying so many products and not seeing any results. It broke my spirit so badly. I know what you're thinking, If your skin was so bad, why didn't you just get some ProActiv and call it a day? I did. I tried everything, but my acne was more complex. I didn't have the common acne-prone skin. After years of studying my acne, I now know my acne was attacking from within. It had nothing to do with my diet or water consumption, and everything to do with hormonal imbalance. I was worried, confused, and more than anything, so embarrassed. Every time I tried a new product, I read: Dermatologists Recommended on the label and this got me so excited, but after several failed attempts, I learned that I didn't have topical acne like most people my age. All the Neutrogena, Cetaphil, Clean and Clear, Aveeno, and Noxzema didn't work! It'll clear my skin for like a week or two, but nothing worked permanently. Whether I stopped eating chocolate, fatty foods, or drank a bunch of water, my skin just wouldn't cooperate!

So after a while, I tried dermatology. Every appointment went the same way. Dermatologists would ask me if I had oily or dry skin, what kind of facial cleansers I used, how often I washed my face, and then offer me some of their most popular cleansers. They would make me feel so encouraged and explain to me how Benzoyl Peroxide, Tazorac, or even birth control worked for so many other people my age. They were sure it would work for me! They'd tell me that if I was consistent, I would see a difference in as little as three months. I figured since I was using stronger products, this would work for sure. I used these products and guess what? Nothing worked. Some of these even caused my skin to get worse!

## *Introduced to Accutane*

I visited my first dermatologist when I was fourteen. From then to now, I'd say I'd been to about five or six different dermatologists. Visiting different dermatologists allowed me to try many skin regimes. I tried topical, foamy soaps, not so foamy soaps, masks, birth controls, pills, creams, facials, nothing was working. After a few repetitive visits, my doctors proposed the idea of trying Accutane. For those who aren't aware, Accutane is a Vitamin A derivative used to treat severe acne. It is ninety-nine percent effective to stop acne from returning. My mom and I did some research, and I probably watched over one hundred reviews on YouTube. You know how after searching

Google; you panic? I swear you can Google something as simple as "mild headache pain" and Google will damn near tell you that you have three months to live and you're suffering from brain cancer. Anyway, after researching people who tried Accutane, we found severe side effects that made me change my mind. Side effects included depression, liver problems, pancreas problems, severe stomach pain, dry skin, cracks on the outside of your mouth, joint pain, back pain, dizziness, drowsiness, and the list goes on! Of course, the idea of having unblemished skin was like a dream, but I wasn't quite ready to go as far as taking Accutane. I hated how I looked, but my mom and I both weren't ready for me to start a drug as strong as Accutane.

So I continued my journey on finding something that worked for me. I told myself that I'd tough it out and still search for something that worked for me. I was still trying new things, still getting the same outcomes. Ultimately, as I got older, my acne was getting worse. So instead of the few years of puberty related acne, normal kids go through, I learned I was suffering from cystic acne. Cystic acne is when the pores in the skin become blocked, leading to infection and inflammation. So my pimples were coming from under the skin. Aside from having active pimples, I had inflammatory scarring. My scars are pretty big and blotchy. When I had active breakouts, my entire face felt swollen. Not only did I have acne on my face , I got cysts in other areas, too. Cysts like my underarms, thighs, breasts, it was horrible. As a young woman, getting cysts on my breasts was extremely scary. A swollen, painful lump on my breasts scared the hell out of me! I didn't know how to explain to my friends what was wrong with me. When I was walking funny, randomly holding my boob just for comfort, or canceling plans because it was too painful to get out of bed, they were curious what was going on, but I would make up some lousy excuse out of embarrassment. This is when I thought something was wrong with me. Cystic acne doesn't just make your appearance look bad, but it is painful. Cysts aren't like pimples. I couldn't just pop them and go about my day. These red, inflamed cysts were below surface level. I would have to get them drained at my local health clinic. I'd walk into the clinic, show them my cysts, they'd make a small incision, and drain it. Extremely painful! I would ask myself, "What am I doing so wrong for my skin to be reacting like this?" Was it my diet, my soaps, my clothes? What the hell was going on with me?

## *A Close-up*

Though it was kind of late in the game, I began documenting my face. I had gotten so used to my skin being filled with marks and bumps that I didn't see the significance in documenting my skin journey, never thinking I would see my skin any differently. Here are some recent photos of my skin.

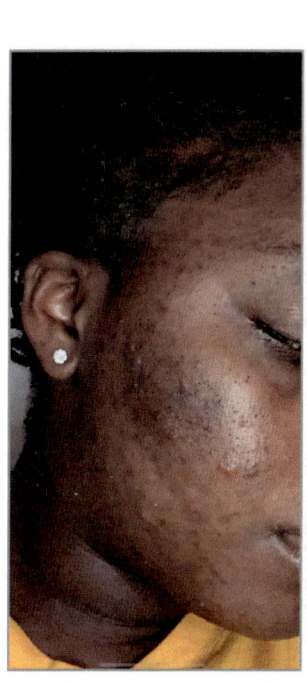
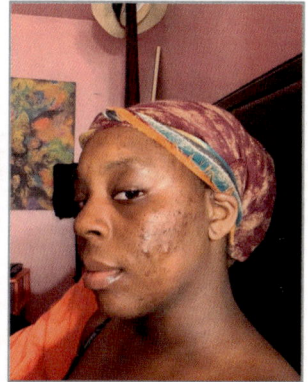
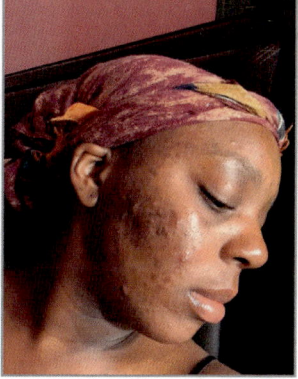

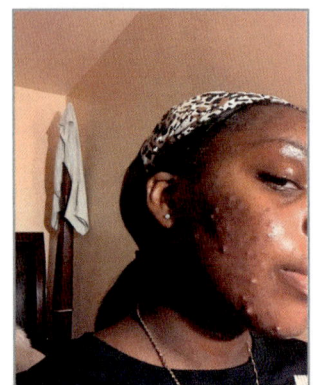
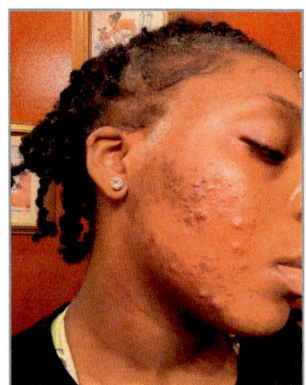
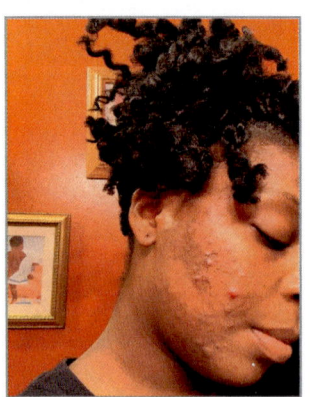
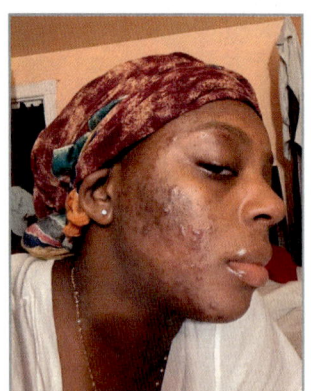
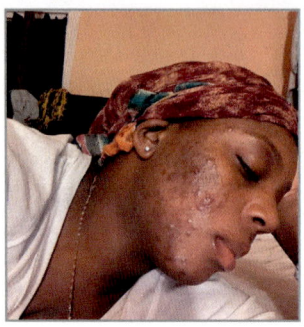

My reality was that I didn't enjoy looking at myself. Anyone with acne knows the pain and suffering of looking at yourself and not being happy. Waking up every day to the same marks and the same pain takes a serious toll on your self-esteem. I saw myself as less than. I saw myself as ugly. What guy would see me as pretty? At the beginning of my days, this was my face. If I put makeup on to feel better and cover-up, I would still see that this was my face beneath. (I wasn't too good at doing my makeup.) By the time I took off that makeup, this was still my face! I wanted clear skin more than anything. I prayed for it, I wanted it so badly. It wasn't always as bad as the photos above. I had some good days, some good moments, but my acne never stayed away. Here are some examples.

 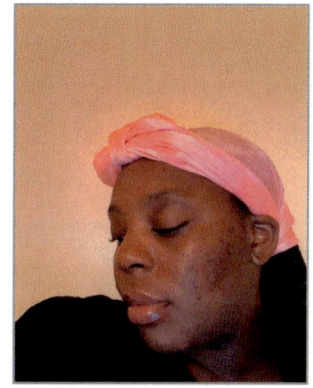

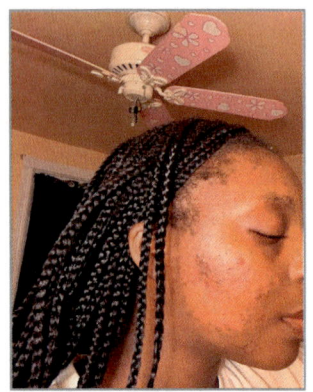 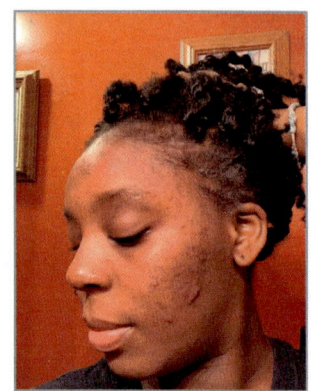

Sometimes people threw that "B" word at me. Not "bitch" but beautiful. For the longest time, I had a hard time accepting this word. I thought people were only calling me that to make me feel better about having acne. Like a, "You have terrible skin but let me tell you you're beautiful anyway," pity compliment kind of thing. I hated those. All I saw was uneven, unclear, bumpy skin and if I saw myself as that I knew for sure others saw me this way, too. Even when I wasn't having a bad skin week, I had scars from previous bumps. I've been battling this for years, always thinking, Is my skin ever gonna get clear? Am I ever going to be as pretty as other girls? Probably not. Am I even pretty?

When I got around boys, I wore my hair in front of my face to cover my blemishes. I would usually not give them eye contact and I'd prefer seeing them at night or in a dark setting like a movie date or late night parked car conversation. I always got so nervous when guys looked me in the eye; I would instantly get offended and look away or change his attention to anything else around that wasn't me. I was so uncomfortable with staring. You know some guys see you for who you are within, but most guys want a beautiful girl and I was not that beautiful girl. At least I didn't think so. So when a guy stares at me, I wanted to know what he was thinking about while staring at me. If I caught a guy staring and ask him why he was looking at me, I would get that infamous, "I can't just look at you?" pick up line. No. Sir. Please don't. If he was thinking anything like what I think when I saw myself, it couldn't be good! With a face as bad as mine, I figured there was no way anyone could think I was beautiful I didn't even think so myself.

## *If you don't, who will?*

How you love yourself is how you teach others to love you. I didn't realize that until I started dating and dealing with guys in my late teenage years. No one is going to show you more respect than you show yourself. I tried to carry myself accordingly, but sometimes my lack of self-love showed. I looked for attention in the wrong places. I was changing myself from that geeky girl to fit in with the crows. I wasn't okay with just being myself, so I talked more "hip." I was walking more stank. I had that little athlete body plus my body was still growing as a teenager, so embarrassingly enough, I was trying to show that off to gain attention from stupid boys in high school and even college to feel better about myself.

My self-esteem was jacked up! It didn't get to a super low point to where I was disrespecting myself. However, I wasn't being myself and that's a low enough point if you ask me. I wasn't even hanging out with that same nerdy clique anymore. I thought I had to be with the popular kids. We weren't even compatible, but I figured if I hung with them I would be a candidate for cute, popular guys. I just wanted to be seen and to feel appreciated. One thing I learned along the way is if you don't appreciate yourself, no one else will. You can't look for self-love by gaining attention and "love" from other people. I wasn't seeing myself as beautiful, so any attention from boys meant they saw something in me I didn't see in myself. Self-love doesn't work that way. If you are bending and conforming to others for self-satisfaction, you will spend a long time looking for your self-love.

# Chapter 4

## WELL, MAYBE IF I...

Not only did having acne physically break me down, it also brought so much emotional distress on me. I was so uncomfortable with looking at myself that I compared myself to just about everyone else around me. Even my friends. "Her shape is amazing, her skin is so clear, her outfit is cute, her hair is so the bomb." My brain compared all day long. Sizing yourself up to others will do nothing but break down the image you have of yourself. Often, and I didn't even mean to, this bad habit that turned into a natural reflex. In today's time, I think it's safe to say we feel the inevitable pressure of keeping up with celebrities and Instagram models. Not just women, men, too! They want to keep up with the flashy rappers that have a bunch of women and a bunch of money. As soon as you log onto social media, models with the perfect shape, rappers with nice cars, and other influencers with stacks of money show up in your news feed. We, regular people, feel like we aren't doing enough almost every time we log onto these apps. Sadly, I had that terrible feeling of not being enough long before the birth of Instagram, Twitter, and Facebook. I saw girls coming to school wearing makeup, and thought, Well, maybe if I cover my bumps I'll be prettier. I saw girls with long silky weaves. Well, maybe if I get a weave, I'll be more attractive. I'm not too ashamed to say I was that girl. I was the girl who looked for acceptance from other people. Newsflash: You cannot find love for yourself while looking at other people. I studied other girls and eventually switched up how I walked, how I talked, and how I carried myself to seem more appealing. Doing this ultimately led to my losing that quirky, bubbly, weird kid. Being a little different and having bad acne just would not work. So, I felt I had to act more like others for others to accept me.

### *No comparison*

Rule number one to this loving yourself thing is f*** what they think! It's all about how you see yourself.

I swear once you get to a point in your life where you solely base your decisions on your judgment, then you've won! Not to say that getting advice and help from others is bad, but when you could care less about what everyone else is doing or looking like, the world is yours! Your only focus should be on you. Don't leave any room to compare yourself to anyone else and never dim your light or switch up your style to be like others. Just to let you know, people are going to talk about you, regardless! You could do good or bad, you could be rich or poor, ugly, beautiful, fat, skinny, whatever. We live in a judgmental world. Sadly. The focus cannot be on others' opinions. It must be on how we see ourselves. I wish I knew back then what I know now. Thinking back, what hurts me the most was that I wasn't that girl comparing herself to others before I had acne. I loved everything about being the geeky kid. It wasn't until I looked at myself in the mirror and was not satisfied that I felt I needed to do other things to enhance my physical appearance. Acne came when the opinions of little sixth-grade boys and those stupid honest direct messages and rates of 1-10 Facebook posts mattered to young girls. I knew none of the boys in my middle school were going to rate me a high number or call me pretty with these bumps on my face. Naturally, I cared about how little middle schoolers saw me and what the popular crew thought of me. Never was I the kid to fit in until acne came and made me feel like I had to do something or I would've just been the geeky kid with bumps on her face. I felt I was the only sixth-grader who was going through what I was going through. It sucked.

### *Girl, what the hell are you doing?*

Comparing yourself to someone else not only causes major damage to your self-esteem, but it can also cause you to make some dumb decisions. Like the time I was fifteen, and I worked at Auntie Anne's in the Cherry Hill Mall. A beautiful girl with honey brown hair came up to me. She was so confident and so beautiful, I wanted to feel that! I would have done just about anything to feel that. So I decided I was going to dye my hair honey brown. Doing this would have made me feel just as pretty as she did. At Least that's what I thought. Well, it was a disaster, and it came out horrible. I asked for honey brown and I got red.

The first mistake in this hair dyeing process was not going to a hair salon that specializes in my coarse,

4C textured hair. The salon I went to had given me a book of color samples. Even though I casually browsed the pages, I knew exactly what I wanted. My mission was to find the color most similar to the girl I saw at work and not something I liked, something I genuinely wanted. No, I was looking for what looked nice on her and hoped it would look nice on me, too. Well, I learned my lesson. Looking back, I envied how beautiful and confident she was when I saw her. I wanted to be that girl. I wanted to feel good about myself like she did, so what the hell, I let them throw the bleach in my hair, damn near burned my scalp, and sent me home with a color I did not ask for. When a stylist finishes, she gives you a mirror and asks if you like it, right? I couldn't even fake the funk. I put the money on her stand and stormed out. As I stood outside and waited for my brother to pick me up, I cried so hard. I was devastated. Not just because the color didn't look right on me, but because I had to deal with the consequences of messing up my beautiful, healthy, unprocessed hair. I had to prepare myself for any ridiculing that was about to come my way. I knew as soon as I stepped foot into school the next day, my "friends" and peers were going to rip me a new one! Which they did.

## *How You See Yourself*

When I was a kid, I loved everything about the arts. I loved singing, dancing, and more than anything in the world, I loved acting. Before acne, I had dreams of being an actress. I took acting classes and vocal lessons every weekend. Once I got older, acne stripped away my confidence, thus vanishing my passion for performing. I didn't want to be seen anymore. I didn't even have the confidence to join theatre in high school. I pushed what I loved to do, what I was born to do, to the side because I didn't believe I was good enough. To remind you, I'd been performing on stage since age two, but having bad acne silenced my dreams. I got weary and shy about acting. I thought I would never be pretty enough to be on stage, that I'd never have the confidence high enough to be on the big screen. So I went off to college and didn't pursue theatre. I settled for communications, knowing damn well that's not what I wanted to do. I went to plays on campus and thought, Wow, I know I can do that, but I'm just too scared.

Recently, I studied Galatians 1:10, "For am I seeking approval of man, or of God? If I were still trying to please man, I would not be a servant of

Christ." I was seeking approval in the wrong places. Today, I try my best not to compare myself to anyone else. I'm not studying how they look, what they have, or what they're doing. It's me vs. me. I encourage you to take the focus off of others and focus on yourself. Invest in yourself. Invest time, energy, peace, and clarity in yourself. I sought approval in all the wrong places. No matter what dumb decisions you've made to seek approval from others, I need you to remember that their judgment should never matter! If you are happy with yourself, that is enough. Once I told myself that I can do all things if I put my mind to it, I joined the theatre company my junior year of college. I loved it. I loved being there, and I loved being around the arts. It was too late to change my major so I did a few auditions and got accepted into two New York acting programs for post-grad. All I had to do was believe in myself! All I had to do was block out the self-doubt in my head. Once I did, my passion for my purpose became clearer. I am currently enrolled in Aikan Performing Arts in Philadelphia, Pennsylvania. I am an aspiring and up-and-coming actress and I know that anything I want to do, I will. I just need to believe in myself! I was so tired of letting acne stand in my way!

*Chapter 5*

## TAKING CARE OF MY MENTAL HEALTH

Your mental health is like the battery in your body. If your battery is low, you feel low. If your battery is charged, you feel good. Like your phone's battery, you can't use those cheap gas station chargers and expect your phone to function at its level best. Use a quality charger to get the best battery. Your mental health is the same way. Charging your body with good essential energy will transfer into how you go about your day. You must keep your battery charged with good actions and good intentions every single day. You've got to wake up every day and chose a great attitude. Attack the day! Keeping your mental health clean, eating right, giving yourself positive affirmations, and surrounding yourself with people who uplift you will put your mental health in a whole different space. Learning how to block out the extra noise was my biggest challenge. I had to teach myself to stop looking at others. I was trying to remind myself that I am beautiful, regardless. I told myself that my quirky personality was just fine. I didn't have to dim my light for any crowd. I'm fine just the way I am.

### *You Need To Cut It!*

You have to make cuts! Friends got to get cut. Habits got to get cut. Shit, some family might have to get cut! Voiding out anything and everything that does not give your battery the energy it needs has to go! Choosing myself over hanging out with others got a little hard for me, only because I'm extremely extroverted, but I needed to put a pause on social engagement and get one hundred percent comfortable being just me! Gradually, I stopped communicating with people who brought nothing but negative vibes around me. I stopped hanging around those who didn't see me for who I am. I stopped answering the phone. I stopped texting back and I was unapologetic about it. I'll tell you now, some moments got lonely. You're going to be tempted to hit up your old friends or your old flings just for a good time but just know by doing so, you are risking the personal growth you need. Sometimes, cut yourself off from the world and learn about yourself. Learn your likes and dislikes. Take yourself out on dates. Treat yourself to a new journal and write out your ideas and goals. Ultimately, having people around is fun and all, but when you're on the road to being the best version of yourself, you need that alone time!

## *Naw, I'm good.*

If it's one thing about the Black community, we think depression and anxiety are a part of life or that we shouldn't seek help or counseling. Most of us don't even care to acknowledge that we or the ones we love are battling serious mental health issues. A lot of us have learned to cope and deal with our issues because we tell ourselves that we have bigger fish to fry or that we can't sit around and bitch and moan about it. That we have to keep going, right? We've been shutting up and "toughing it out" for years. According to the Columbia Psychiatry Organization, the adult Black community is twenty percent more likely to go through mental health issues, especially anxiety and depression compared to anyone else. Sadly, compared to white adults, Black adults between the ages of eighteen and twenty-five receive fewer mental health services. Some common reasoning why young Black adults may experience anxiety and depression is because of social injustices, poverty, lack of trust in the medical system, and/or financial burden. We could list so many reasons Black adults don't seek help for their mental health issues, but that's not what I wish to do. Whether you are Black, white, Spanish, Asian, Indian, it doesn't matter! Mental health is extremely important in all of us. Acknowledging mental health issues is the first step to changing your life. Doing this could save your life.

Speaking from experience and growing up in an urban community, I know some issues that minorities face. I see it every day. I also know there are resources available to help those in need, but you have to be willing to receive them. A wise woman (my mom) once told me that you cannot help someone if they do not want to be helped. As instrumental as mental health is to me, I can lead you to water, but I can't make you drink. Knowing what my fellow brothers and sisters go through, I would love it if we took better care of our mental health. I wanted to make sure I highlighted mental health in the Black community because, for me, it was hard to seek help. It was hard for me to realize I needed help. I thought I was good, I was fine, I didn't need any counselor telling me what was wrong with me. I know many people in my community think this way, which is why the Black community's mental health statistics are where they are now. However, even if you are reading this and you are not a person of color, please, please, please seek help if you are struggling mentally. We all need to do better jobs of taking care of ourselves.

### *Find Your Mind*

Do you want to know what I realized when I was going through it mentally? If your mind is suffering, your physical health will suffer as well. There are several physical effects on the body when someone is suffering from anxiety. Some include fatigue, panic attacks, headaches, irritability, breathing problems, muscle aches, and loss of libido. Another long list of physical effects on the body when dealing with depression is weight fluctuations, constricted blood vessels, trouble with memory and decision making, insomnia, and a weakened immune system. Our bodies and minds work together! If you are not good mentally, how could you expect your body to stay afloat physically? We need to stop living in this stigma that seeking help is weakness. What's weak is burying and distracting your issues in other people, drugs, and alcohol. That's weak. It takes a strong individual to say, "I'm not okay" or "I need help." It took me years, but realizing I wasn't okay was the best thing I'd ever done. Newsflash: you're human. You don't always have to be okay.

Getting my first taste of depression and anxiety my freshman year of college was odd. I say odd because anyone who looked at me or hung with me wouldn't have been able to realize what I was going through. Normal freshmen in college go out, experience thirsty Thursdays, skip class a few times, and have break nights with their friends. While I did all of that (besides the whole skip class part), I hid my depression and anxiety from my friends and family. Going out and distracting myself from my issues was my strategy, and it worked! It was all fun and games when I was pre-gaming in my dorm, throwing on a crop top pop (in any weather), biker shorts, and vans.

41

Parties. (My favorite part of those nights were when we all sat at a local diner and waited for our drunk to wear off, all while eating breakfast food at 3:00 a.m.) However, when I got back to my room, I wasn't happy. I wasn't even really happy while I was out. I was just drunk! I was distracting myself and my brain from what bothered me. When I had those moments alone, I spent my time in my dark dorm, crying. I had no desire to eat, and bathing was a necessity, but I had no desire to get dolled up or pretty. I didn't do my hair or makeup. I just wanted to go to class, get drunk, and drown all my insecurities on the weekends with a $13 bottle of New Amsterdam. (Don't judge me; we all started somewhere during our freshman year of college.) Somehow, filling myself up with this poison, and I do mean poison, made me feel better.

First thing is first. Find your mind. Take the time to feel what you're going through. Believe me, it's okay to feel! It is one hundred percent okay to not be okay. We're human! What's not okay is burying your feelings and faking the funk. I did that for too long. I wasn't quite ready to look my insecurities in the face. I didn't want to attack them head-on. I somehow wanted them to disappear magically, but drowning them in New Amsterdam would not do the job. It was extremely important for me to separate myself from those people who weren't contributing to my feeling better. Do everything for a reason. Everything needs a purpose. Just like people in your life. Everyone in your life needs a purpose, too!

# *Chapter 6*

## Unapologetically

**Jump!**

Ever since I could remember, my mom has told me that listening to my instinct could save my life someday. She told me that each time I felt something in my spirit; it was God speaking to me and I needed to never ignore it. Mostly, I did a pretty good job of listening to God in tough times. Listening to Him when He said, "Naw, don't go to that party" or "Naw, don't hang out with that crew anymore." I picked up on His messages pretty clearly. It's weird, but God speaks to me in my dreams. He'll talk to me while I'm sleeping and I'm pretty sure it's because He knows my days are always so busy and He wants my undivided attention to hear His messages.

One random morning in October 2017, I woke up with Norfolk State University heavy on my mind. I knew nothing about Norfolk State. I only knew one person from high school who went there, and I had been to Virginia one time, but that was about it. Why did this school randomly pop in my head? It was weird. So on this day, I woke up confused and something just told me to Google the school. From there, I did some research and thought, Wow, this is where I need to be. Thank goodness for social media. I started following students, student leaders, student athletes, and even just random Norfolk State people just to get a little virtual view of what to expect. After YouTubing past homecoming and other events, I was sold. I instantly fell in love with this illustrious university.

Something in my head was telling me to just go! Apply and leap out on faith. That something was my instinct! Not listening to your instinct can be so self-sabotaging. You have got to be able to hear your gut feeling. It sounds crazy, but being distracted by a million different things going on, will cause you to miss your moment. Let me say it again for the people that may need to hear me again: you will miss your moment being too busy to receive it. Too busy with work. Too busy with your relationship. Too busy with family drama. Your moment and gut feeling may be here one minute and gone the next. Ultimately, it was time to leave Kean University and get a fresh start. I was too comfortable. Comfortability will have you stuck! God woke me up and told me that there's something out there for me! Going back and forth with Him, because of doubt and insecurity, is like arguing with God. Dontcha think? If God put this school in my head with zero resonance with this school, and I brushed it to the side or undoubtedly moved this idea to the back of my head, wouldn't that be like us questioning His judgement?

So I applied, packed all of my things, and left Kean. Over the three weeks of winter break, I had zero direction of where I would be in school the following January. I didn't want to go back to Kean, and I had the credentials to transfer to Norfolk State, but they weren't accepting me fast enough. (No shade, but HBCU financial aid offices…y'all know how that goes.) I was very insecure and wary about my decision because I wasn't getting any responses. I didn't let that discourage me. I was persistent. When you set your mind on a goal, don't lose sight of it! I set an alarm on my phone every day at 8:00 a.m. sharp to call Norfolk State's financial aid and admissions to get a straightforward answer on what my next move would be. Then boom, after about two-and-a-half weeks of no answers and being on hold for hours at a time, I finally got an answer. I got accepted! I didn't even have a housing assignment when a lady at the office said, "Baby, drive down to Norfolk. I'll see you in the morning. I don't have a housing assignment for you yet, but I promise, we will not leave you out in the cold." That's all I needed to hear. I told my friends, I told my family, and I got to packing. See, when you're about to go through a life change, many people won't understand your why. Trust me, my friends and parents were looking at me like, "Wait, you're moving where? Why?" Never let the doubt and confusion of others take you off your track. I didn't have any answers for everyone when they asked me why I was going six hours away to go to school. All I knew was that I had a calling, and I had to listen to Him. God's timing, God's way, not mine.

I share this story with you because I had no idea the impact Norfolk State University was going to have on my life. I was unprepared for everything that NSU offered. No one warned me of preparing for the lessons, friendships, and experiences that this university gave to me. What I knew was I needed to be in a better headspace. I needed to stop hanging out, partying so much, and I needed to listen to myself! Unmute myself, understand that my lack of self-confidence was causing me to self-destruct. I was ready to let that confident leader that was screaming inside of me out. It was time to grow into a leader. I didn't want to party anymore. I didn't care for wasting my time with college guys. I wanted to grow into somebody! I didn't want to go home with just a college degree. I wanted the full experience.

My parents had their doubts, but ultimately I knew if I didn't just leap and go I would never know what was out there for me. Granted, when I arrived at Norfolk State University in January, 2018 I was very uncomfortable. I didn't know anybody, and I didn't know the area. I was in a place I had never been before looking for a new start. Sometimes being a little uncomfortable is all it takes! In May 2020, I graduated from the illustrious Norfolk State University with a 3.8 overall GPA and several accolades and leadership positions under my belt. Best decision ever!

If you are contemplating leaping out on faith because you are fearful, remember that you'll never know how it'll turn out if you don't go for it. Even if it fails, at least you can say you tried. Never know that one leap can change your life in so many ways. Norfolk State taught me the importance of being confident, being a leader, and always following my dream. I got back into what I loved most, performing, and the best thing I learned at Norfolk State was how to love myself again.

## Chapter 7

## FLOAT LIKE A BUTTERFLY

Ever since I was a kid, I've had an obsession with butterflies. It's not until now that I realized why I've always loved them. Not only have I always admired their uniqueness in the way they look, but I'm obsessed with their evolution. Beginning as an egg, forming into a caterpillar, drying into their cocoons, then spreading their wings into beautiful butterflies.

Butterflies aren't born being those confident little creatures. It's a process. When you're ready to break through that shell and float like a butterfly, you will. I'm not going to lie, with changing my lifestyle, I was hesitant and inconsistent. I wasn't ready to float. When you decide to change your situation, you'll start seeing different results. It's mind over matter, honestly. Speak it, write it out, and practice good habits to see results.

## *Your Lane Only*

I ran track for a good portion of my life. The most important lesson I learned was how to run a race of my own. I learned the importance of running my race even when off of the track. In the eighth grade, my first coach introduced me to how important it was to not give up. I couldn't focus on who was next to me. I couldn't focus on what was going on behind me. I had to stay in my lane. I had to block out the background noise. Your lane may get lonely. It may even be a challenge, but when you're challenging your life, your new lane may become uncomfortable that you're tempted to revert to your old lane and habits. Growth takes discipline! You know what they say, consistency is key. Sounds cliché, but it's so true! Consistency is the main ingredient to changing your lifestyle. One thing I learned along the way was when you've had enough of feeling a certain way, being a certain way, and receiving a certain energy, then that's when you'll be ready for change. Talk is cheap. You can talk about how much you're ready to lose weight until you're blue in the face. You can even talk about how tired you are of dealing with certain friends or partners all you want, but it won't be until you are ready to change your habits within when you will be ready for different outcomes. It takes willpower. It's that simple.

I was one of those people who would go on little diets, cleanses, and detoxes for a certain amount of time and I would fake like I was just a new person, but eventually, I would go right back to square one. I lacked willpower. It takes willpower to start a new habit. Takes mental strength and discipline to stay consistent. According to health psychologists, it takes about twenty-one days to form a habit. Some say it's a myth, and it takes more, but I think one can make a habit in as little as twenty-one days, or less. If I wake up at 6:00 a.m. every morning and go to the gym for twenty-one days, it'll get easier and become my everyday routine. My biggest issue with committing to something is not getting to where I made it a part of my routine. A wise man by the name of Eric Thomas once said, "When you wanna be successful as bad as you wanna breathe, then you'll be successful." Trust me, you won't get anywhere awaiting results to just magically fall into your lap. I know I will not get rid of this acne and weight until I eat better, take better care of my body and mind, sleep better, and stay consistent with whatever regime that works for me. It may take some time but good food cooks slow, be patient.

The first step I took into switching gears and changing my situation was surrounding myself with more positive individuals. This is so important. Sometimes, surrounding yourself with better vibes means spending more time alone. Being a social butterfly wasn't always easy, but I had to protect my energy. Everyone doesn't deserve you or your energy. Ultimately, when you're moving on in your life, everyone doesn't make it with you. This means relationships may end or friendships may become distant. Don't feel bad about it. Even when people try to confront you on how you may act differently, stand your ground and stay true to your goal. Many people who aren't ready to grow will not understand what you're doing. Your "why" is for you only. It's not your job to make them understand it. As long as you believe in yourself, you are going to reach any goal to which you aspire. If you want to change something about yourself, don't talk about it, be about it! Stay confident and trust me, you will see results.

# *Chapter 8*

## EVERY. DAMN. DAY.

I don't think people without acne understand the emotional toll having acne has on those with acne. The battle is much bigger than physical! I'll be the first to tell you that emotionally, I've been messed up for years. Having acne has made me feel so hopeless for so long. I had a hard time loving myself, which led into my struggle with loving others, which led to the struggle of accepting love, which ultimately led to lots of lonely nights and self-doubt. There were many nights I would cry myself asleep because I knew that when I woke up in the morning, I'd still be fighting the same fight. The thing about acne is no matter how many people feel bad for you and say they understand what you're going through, the fight is yours.

I had to endure this alone. I walked my eleven years of cystic alone every day by myself. No one else felt what I felt when I looked into the mirror. No one else felt as defeated as I did when I tried everything to clear my skin up. I didn't talk about it with my friends, I didn't tweet about it, this was between me and me. There were hundreds of times when my mom would feel just as hopeless as I did because she knew there was nothing she could do to make me feel better. All she could do was loan me a shoulder, grab me some tissues, and fill me up with encouraging words. My mom has always been so comforting and emotionally available for me when I needed it. I appreciate her being there so much but ultimately, my mom didn't make this pain go away. I would sit on the school bus and mentally note that I had about ten to twelve minutes to get myself together before I got to school and the "What's wrong with you?" questions would start rolling in. I would sit outside of work or clock in and rush right to the bathroom to look myself in the mirror and tell myself it's gonna be okay. Doing this was so hard.

### *How are you gonna tell me what's on my face?*

I'm sure just about everyone has had a stubborn pimple or two in their lifetime but dealing with severe acne that just wouldn't go away put my confidence in the trash. It was my face! It was the first thing I saw when I woke up in the morning. It was the first thing people saw when they looked at me. Acne had the power to make a great day, bad. It had the power to turn a good mood or moment, sour with just one glance. Whether or not I knew them personally I knew they were looking and criticizing me. Acne made me feel so small, so less than. I felt like I had to stay quiet when discussing beauty with other girls. I felt I had to keep my opinions to myself when discussing skin or healthy routines. Who the hell was going to take tips from a girl with skin like mine? Acne isn't something that I could just take off or cover up, this was me. For years. People stared, some called me names, some got real close to my face making me feel alienated! Some even called themselves inserting their lousy two cents about my skin, as if I didn't see my face. To anyone who struggles with acne, I want you to know I feel your pain. I have felt your pain every single day for eleven years. I know all about the nights you cry yourself to sleep, been there. I know all about not wanting to go out because you feel ugly. I know all about feeling ugly! Trust me. I want you to know that acne is a pain in the ass that you will get through! We will get through this. I promise. To those without acne, be patient and gentle with those with it. Be very delicate with us because we already feel small about how we look. We already feel like the odd ball please try not to single us out and shine a spotlight on us for having it. We've tried everything! Stop telling us to eat better, to drink more water, to wash our pillow cases or to try the skin care routine that works for you, for some of us it isn't that simple! As much as you want to see their skin clear, imagine that times one hundred. There was nothing I wanted more than to wake up one day and just see my skin clear. Acne doesn't have an age, my mom told me in 2009 that I would grow out of it. A decade later, I'm still struggling with it. I had no hope that my skin was ever going to look different. I got so comfortable with my skin being so terrible.

Living with acne every day was challenging, to say the least. I was awkward around boys, I felt awkward when girls would put makeup on around me, and it made me extremely uncomfortable when people would criticize their almost perfect skin like, c'mon look at me! Be grateful! I just felt out of the ordinary. I struggled with hyperpigmentation, a bunch of scars, and big pimples. It wasn't easy to hide. I wasn't comfortable in my own skin. I would wake up every day and prepared myself for the world. Whether that meant throwing on some foundation, covering my face with my hair (which probably only clogged my pores even more), I would just do anything to prepare for another day of not loving how I looked. Sounds dramatic, but it's true. For so many people COVID-19 has ruined lives but for me, having to wear a mask covering my terrible skin every day in all places was good news. I was so happy to wear them around people at work and around friends. It gave me an opportunity to hide without seeming like the shy uncomfortable girl. To others I was following state guidelines but to me, I was hiding my skin from the world. Covering my truth, hiding behind a mask that I wish I had years prior. This way no one couldn't judge me for my flaws. Wearing a mask no one could see my imperfections, my acne was between me and me and that was the best feeling ever. I sure could've used these face masks back when I was in high school!

# *Chapter 9*

## CREATING A NEW NORM

### *Do It Differently*

In October 2020, it was time to quit talking. I'd had enough of being unhappy with the way I looked. I'd had enough of being unhappy with the way I felt. Here's a head's up. You aren't getting any younger! Another day is an opportunity to better yourself. I knew if I didn't change some habits I was going to be stuck in self-doubt forever! I didn't have any excuses to throw out there to comfort myself anymore. I was the only one in my way! School was done, I had no love life, my social life had slowed down a lot since I'd been home, my job wasn't too demanding, so it was the perfect time to pour into myself. I had time to scroll up and down social media for hours, right? I had time to go out and spend money on myself from time to time, right? If I had time to do other things, I had time to invest in feeling better. I was so tired of not loving the reflection that stared back at me. I hated it for years! I'd had enough.

It was finally time to leap. I marched down to Center City Dermatology, shared with them my struggle with acne, and how eager I was to get started with Accutane. After watching so many Accutane journey videos on YouTube and reading different stories, I learned that this drug is not for the weak. I was fearful, but if this was what it was going to take to clear me up; I was ready to leap! Because this drug is so strong, a dermatologist doesn't just start you on it. They want to make sure you've tried other medicines before. I was pretty nervous about what my dermatologist would tell me, but she was one hundred percent on board with my getting started as soon as possible, and I couldn't have been happier. I hugged the doctor! I was so ecstatic! I got all my blood work done and began my Accutane journey on October 13, 2020.

Along with getting my skin on the right track, I was ready to develop healthier habits into my daily routine.

Not only was I obsessed to look good, but to feel good on the outside was the ultimate goal. So many people in today's generation are flashy, materialistic, worried about their appearance, and as much as that means to me, being that I hadn't loved the way I looked for so long, I was eager to feel good internally. I was so ready to just get to a point of comfort with myself. It was time to create a new normal. I ate healthier, cut down on fried foods, lessened the amount of sugar intake, I was more consistent with exercising, started my days earlier, read more books, and cut down on my social media presence and activity. I was developing a new attitude! I learned how to stop looking at and comparing myself to others, how to find my own beauty, my own identity. I learned how to love and appreciate myself. On the inside and out. The main focus for me was to stop being so hard on myself. I learned to share and celebrate my achievements. I stayed motivated and hopeful for a better tomorrow. I was feeling better. Mentally and physically.

For the longest time, I was so caught up in others and their successes. Others and their happiness. Others and their beauty. I was letting mine slip away. How can you fully focus on yourself while you're worried about the next person? You write your own story, so when you're ready to buckle down and make some sacrifices to be a better you, then you will. Stop making excuses. Stop lying to or distracting yourself to feel better temporarily. You are most accountable for your present and future, so don't let anyone, anything, or even your own doubts stand in the way of that. Write out your plans. Write your goals. Set reminders. Pray even! Whatever you have to do, get to where your new routine is uncomfortable, it doesn't feel right, a point where it feels weird, because that's when you'll know you're doing something different. Make time for yourself! Pour into yourself. Don't wait on anybody to do it for you.

## *Chapter 10*

### ALWAYS REMEMBER

If there's anything you need to take from this book, it is to remember you are enough. Say goodbye to self-doubt! Every day, remind yourself you are beautiful inside and out! You are able. You are healthy. You are different. You are worth it. After years of not knowing who I was, after taking different routes to figure out my purpose and worth, I know today that anything I put my mind to, I can do. "I can do all things through Christ who strengthens me." That Bible verse, Philippians 4:13, is so important to me now. I was the only one holding me back. I was the only one standing in my way of growing. God will strengthen you to do anything you want to do! The sooner you take your eyes off of others and gain a stronger into a relationship with yourself and with Him is when you will progress. I promise. You must surround yourself with those who want better for you! Remember, it may get lonely.

Every day I need to charge my battery with good thoughts if I want to be successful. You do not wake up to be mediocre. You wake up to fulfill a purpose. It's okay if you're still trying to figure out what that purpose may be. No one else can tell you what's best for you. From now on, I won't let anyone else's opinions or critique define me. I owe it to myself to always keep in my mind: I AM ENOUGH. In every room I walk into, I belong there. I wear my confidence. I've dealt with feeling like I was ugly, unworthy, and simply not good enough for so long. Those days are over! Self-worth is not something that I woke up with. It took years of crying, years of timidness, years of comparing myself to realize I had to find my self-worth on my own. Today when I look into the mirror, blemishes or not, I know my skin does not define my beauty. I'm a beautiful person. A beautiful individual with a gift and a purpose God gave me to fulfill. I shall not be in doubt anymore.

The world we are living in today will make you feel less than for not having the tangible things that everyone else has. While all those things are nice, I have something I never want to lose—myself. I refuse to allow society's standards to define me. Count me out. The world will have to deal with a quirky personality and a few pimples because I shall not feel like I don't belong anymore. Today I'm comfortable being me. Do not give any job, relationship, friendship, or family member control over your worth. You're the only one with that power.

Made in the USA
Middletown, DE
16 February 2021

33878931R00038